ENGLISH CIVIL WAR

A History From Beginning to End

Copyright © 2016 by Hourly History

Table of Contents

Introduction

During the time of the English Civil Wars the three kingdoms involved - England, Scotland and Ireland - were sparsely populated. For the ordinary people of these three kingdoms, the outbreak of war may have been little more than an inconvenience, a row between their masters that had little effect on their daily lives. But what began as a series of disagreements between King Charles I and the English Parliament developed into an armed struggle - a full-scale revolution that affected every person in the three kingdoms and took the lives of an estimated 800,000 individuals.

The English Civil Wars were fuelled by conflicts that had taken hold in Scotland and Ireland in the years preceding. The Bishops' Wars in Scotland and the Ulster Rebellion in Ireland exacerbated tensions between Charles I and Parliament, and although the Civil War ravaged England beyond comprehension, it also devastated the other two kingdoms held by the House of Stuart. For this reason the English Civil Wars could easily be called the Wars of the Three Stuart Kingdoms.

Officially the first English Civil War was fought between 1642 and 1646; the second began in 1648 and resulted in the shocking execution of the king; the third took place between 1649 and 1651. The third English Civil War culminated in the new king fleeing into exile and the establishment of the Commonwealth of England, a government that soon found itself under Oliver

Cromwell's personal rule. The Parliamentary army's victory over the King forever changed the English constitution as well as the role of the Monarchy and Parliament would play across the British Isles.

Chapter One

Reasons to go to War

"Princes are not bound to give an account of their Actions but to God alone"

—King Charles I of England, Scotland and Ireland

In 1603, the era of the Tudors in England came to an end and the era of the Stuarts began. On March 24th, Queen Elizabeth I died and her thrones passed to her cousin King James VI of Scotland, who became King James I of England and Ireland. For the very first time, the three separate kingdoms of England, Ireland and Scotland were united under one king. Maintaining peace across these very different kingdoms would not be easy for James, as there was a long and bloody history of conflict between the kingdoms; animosity ran deep.

The three kingdoms differed in their attitude towards the monarchy and the state. As King of Scotland, James enjoyed a great deal of power; he was able to exercise much control over the Scottish parliament and lived with few restraints. Upon taking over the English throne, James was surprised and incensed by the limitations the English parliament placed on his power and their restrictions on his access to the country's treasury. Long known as an extravagant king prone to splendour and excess, James was constantly short of cash and became frequently frustrated by Parliament's refusal to give in to his demands for funds.

All three kingdoms also practiced a different dominant religion. The English were predominantly Protestant while most Scottish citizens were Calvinist and the Irish were primarily Catholic. Within each kingdom there was also a number of influential religious minorities that further complicated this precarious melting pot of faith.

In England the tension between Protestants and Catholics had reached fever pitch during the reign of King Henry VIII. In 1534, with the help of his chief minister Thomas Cromwell, Henry passed the Acts of Supremacy, declaring himself as "the only supreme head on earth of the Church of England". By doing so, Henry had effectively replaced the Pope as the head of the church in England. Later, Henry passed a further Act in Restraint of Appeals, abolishing the right of citizens to appeal to Rome against the king, a move that saw him excommunicated from the Catholic Church. At this time Catholicism was effectively outlawed in England and the persecution and execution of English Catholics was rife. This persecution continued throughout the 16th century, halting briefly under the rule of Queen Mary Tudor (also known as 'Bloody Mary') and then continuing throughout the reign of Queen Elizabeth I, who was herself a committed protestant.

Before becoming king in England and Ireland, James had promised to adopt a tolerant stance on religion, stating that he would not persecute anyone unless they broke the law. However, James did not follow through on his promise and once he became king he persecuted English Catholics just as severely as before. In 1605, disillusioned by James' false promises and determined to be heard, a group of Catholic conspirators hatched the famous Gunpowder Plot. The scheme, which planned to blow up the Houses of Parliament with King James inside, ultimately failed; however, it served as a dramatic wake-up call to the dangers of ruling a country that is divided along religious lines.

Despite the dramatic events of 1605, James' reign was a time of relative peace across the three kingdoms. James had sought throughout his reign to keep his recently-united kingdoms out of foreign conflicts. However, in the later years of his reign - and due to complications arising from the marriage of his daughter Elizabeth to Frederick V, elector of the Rhineland Palatinate - James unwittingly dragged England, Scotland and Ireland into what became the Thirty Years' War.

In 1625, King James I of England died and King Charles I, his second son, ascended to the throne. In the early years of his rule, Charles succeeded in alienating many of his peers and subjects. Already an unpopular figure with a reputation for being severe and arrogant, Charles inherited the Duke of Buckingham as his principal Minister. If Charles was unpopular in parliament then Buckingham was practically detested. Unfortunately Charles did not inherit his father's desire for peace and, under instruction from Buckingham, threw his kingdoms whole-heartedly into the ongoing fight against Catholic forces on the continent.

War is not cheap, and Charles demanded a large sum of money from the House of Commons in 1625 to fund the war effort, a demand that was not met. Suspicious of Charles' recent marriage to a French Roman Catholic princess, Henrietta Maria, Parliament feared Charles was siding with the Roman Catholics and tried to put a stop to his war effort by denying him funds.

During 1626 and 1627, without the financial support of Parliament, Buckingham orchestrated a number of disastrous attacks on the continent. The House of Commons continued to reject Charles' repeated appeals for money, and as a result England's involvement in the Thirty Years' War was financed by new and unpopular taxes. These taxes, which an enraged Parliament deemed illegal, alarmed the landowners of England who now believed that their private property may be under threat from their own king. Buckingham was later assassinated, supposedly by a fanatic, but the damage to Charles' reputation and the economy of his kingdoms was already done.

Charles' attitude towards his role as king mirrored that of his father, James. Charles believed in the "Divine Right of Kings", that all kings were "little gods on Earth" and that his power over his kingdoms was absolute. This is the attitude that Charles took to the House of Commons on 10th March 1629, the first of his major run-ins with Parliament. Three resolutions were passed by Parliament that day. The first stated that anyone who introduced religious innovations to the Church was a capital enemy of the kingdom. The second, that anyone who allowed the levying of tonnage and poundage (import and export tax) without Parliament's explicit consent was a capital enemy of the kingdom and the third, that any merchant who paid these duties was a "betrayer of the liberties of England". When the House of Commons broke up on 10th March 1629 they had no idea that they were not to meet for another 11 years; in response to Parliament's attempt to curb his authority as king, Charles dissolved parliament and ruled for 11 years by decree, a period that later became known as Charles' Personal Rule (1629-1640).

During this period, Charles became steadily more unpopular with his subjects across his three kingdoms. In order to generate income, Charles resorted to reviving a tax that had not been seen since Elizabethan times. The "ship money" levy, as it was known, was an annual tax on seaports and coastal towns that were collected to pay for the Royal Navy. In 1635, Charles applied this tax to inland towns and began collecting it from any citizen who had the means to pay. Parliament and tax-paying citizens were aghast at what they considered an arbitrary tax being collected illegally by the king. In the same year, Charles introduced a series of ecclesiastical reforms in England. Charles' Queen, Henrietta Maria of France, was openly Catholic, as was William Laud, Charles' close personal adviser and the archbishop of Canterbury. Many English Protestants, particularly the more zealous puritans, were suspicious of the increase in "popery" in England and feared that Charles was trying to restore the Catholic faith.

It is possible that Charles could have endured his unpopularity and enjoyed a long and peaceful reign over his three kingdoms had it not been for the 1637 Scottish uprising. Charles had made the disastrous decision to introduce a modified version of the English Book of Common Prayer in Scotland. The young king had already enraged a number of Scots by interfering with Scottish land titles, and now he was trying to interfere with the Scottish people's religion. This would not stand; a wave of violent riots broke out across Scotland and a National Covenant – a radical call to arms against Charles' Personal Rule – was drawn up. A revolution was on its way.

Charles sent an English army to put the Scottish rebels in their place but the Covenanters, as the rebels were known, were militarily superior to the English army and easily defeated them in what is now known as the First Bishops' War. Despite signing a peace treaty with the Covenanters in June 1639 Charles refused to be beaten; in desperation he recalled English Parliament to raise the funds he needed for another war. It had been 11 years since the last Parliament had met, and while the House of Commons agreed to hand over the money Charles needed, their generosity came with certain conditions. Charles was furious at the list of Parliament's demands and grievances about his behavior, much of which dated back to the last time Parliament was in effect. Again,

Charles dissolved the English Parliament, this time after just three weeks of recall.

The Second Bishops' War was an even greater disaster for Charles. The Covenanters invaded England on August 28th, 1640, and took control of the town of Newcastle following their victory at the Battle of Newburn. Now thoroughly humiliated and with no money to improve his army, the king was forced to recall Parliament for the second time.

Meanwhile in Ireland, Charles' representative Thomas Wentworth was fuelling another rebellion. In 1633, Charles had made Wentworth the lord deputy of Ireland, and Wentworth's plan for the emerald isle was simple: to suppress any belief or activity that did not serve the purposes of the English crown. Wentworth's policies sought to force all Irish subjects to conform to the Church of England, to assert the crown's authority over Irish lands by establishing British plantations and, finally, to "civilize" the Irish people. A nation already severely divided along religious lines, Ireland's Protestants and Catholics were briefly united in their joint hatred of Wentworth and his governance.

When Charles recalled Parliament on November 3rd, 1640, he unwittingly united the Protestant and Catholic elite of Ireland, the Scottish Covenanters and all English opponents of the king. These three factions of the Stuart kingdom joined together to impeach Thomas Wentworth, now the Earl of Strafford, and condemn him to death. Once their joint enemy had been eliminated, Irish Catholic natives and English and Scottish Protestant settlers turned back to face each other as the root of all of their grievances. The ensuing Ulster Uprising of 1641 was a bloody massacre, during which it is believed thousands of ordinary citizens were murdered.

The immediate problem of how to suppress militant Irish rebels is believed to be the primary spark that lit the fire of the first English Civil War. Charles and his Parliament could not agree on who should be in control of the army they needed to raise in order to bring peace back to Ireland. Parliament demanded that Charles employs only those ministers approved by Parliament and that Parliament, not the monarchy, should henceforth control the military. Charles could not allow such an extreme rebuttal of his powers as king, and in retaliation he removed a number of high-standing officials from their posts and issued a new declaration on religion. This disagreement quickly escalated into preparation for war; without the agreement of Parliament, Charles mobilized an army of his own, raising his standard in Nottingham on August 22nd, 1642.

At first it seemed that Charles had few supporters. The majority of the English nobility and landed gentry were reluctant to pledge allegiance so early in the war but there were those who believed in the "Divine Right of Kings" and supported Charles' innovations in the Church. On the other hand, Charles had alienated many with his actions in the Thirty Years' War, his arbitrary taxes, his clashes with Parliament and what was perceived as his betrayal of the Protestant Church. The ruling classes were effectively split down the middle: the stage was set for the first English Civil War.

Chapter Two

The First English Civil War: Choose Your Side

"If there is a single trait in our character that has historically set us apart from other nations, it is our determination to limit the authority of those who rule over us."

—Billy Bragg, 'The Progressive Patriot'

In the lead up to the first major battle of the English Civil War, both sides scrambled to recruit as many men as possible. On one side were the Royalists, those loyal to King Charles I, who would also come to be known as the "Cavaliers", a term derived from the Spanish word Caballeros meaning horsemen. On the other side were the Parliamentarians, those in support of Parliament, soon nicknamed the "Roundheads", so called for the shaved heads adopted by many of the young London apprentices who came out in support of Parliament.

Many factors had to be taken into consideration when deciding which side to support in the first English Civil War, above and beyond whether or not you owned a horse and how you wore your hair. Class was an important factor in determining your allegiance. The rise of the Parliamentarians threatened the established social order, and it was in the best interests of the elite - the peerage and the gentry - to support whichever side would retain the status quo. Those who were blessed with the favor of the king wished to stay in that state of grace, and many may have felt bound to the king by personal loyalty. However, it was much harder to determine allegiance based on class amongst the lower echelons of society. It's possible that there were as many Royalists as there were Parliamentarians amongst the lower gentry and that factors other than class had influenced their decision.

For some lower class subjects the decision of which side to support may have been made for them. In the scramble to take up arms in order to enjoy the financial reward of a soldier's pay and the potential for plunder, many men may have joined whichever army turned up in their village first. Hundreds of foreign mercenaries flocked to England when news spread across the world that the country was at war, and many men were forced to join the war against their will. Tenants were forced to fight for their landlords and men picked up by the local constable could be forced to join the passing army at gunpoint.

Religion also played a significant role in many individual's decision of which side to fight for. Religious conservatives, those who had been raised within the Church of England, were keen to keep the church as it was, while those who were more zealously Protestant wanted to rid the church of all traces of Catholicism. Religious conservatives turned to the Royalists and those who sought religious revolution largely turned to the Parliamentarians.

Alongside religion, the kingdoms of England, Scotland and Ireland could be effectively divided over notions of ethnicity. Parliament portrayed itself as the very epitome of Englishness, an image that was popular throughout the majority of England but led to a backlash in the west of the country. The people of Cornwall and Wales identified as Celtic and aligned themselves with the king throughout the entire conflict. Charles used the Parliamentarian's alienating claims of "superior Englishness" against them and brought soldiers over from Ireland to support his cause. Paradoxically the majority of the Scots sided with Parliament, a phenomenon that led some English to develop anti-Scottish sentiments and defect to the King's side later in the conflict.

Chapter Three

The First English Civil War: The War Begins

""I never could believe that Providence had sent a few men into the world, ready booted and spurred to ride, and millions ready saddled and bridled to be ridden.""

—Richard Rumbold

Since the beginning of 1642, both the Royalist and Parliamentary armies had been scrambling to recruit the greatest number of soldiers and equip them with everything they would need to win a war. The Parliamentary army, serving under the command of the Earl of Essex, was likely the most formidable. Having served as a general in the Netherlands, Essex knew how to lead an army and had six cavalry regiments, 19 infantry regiments and five troops of dragoons - a total of around 15,000 men - at his disposal. Thanks to his massive personal wealth, the earl was able to arm and pay his soldiers extremely well. By comparison the King was acting as his own commander-in-chief and had at his disposal eight cavalry regiments, fifteen infantry and one troop of dragoons for a slightly lower total of around 13,500 men.

At the outbreak of war most of the troops on both sides were under-prepared. As the first campaigns had begun around harvest time, there was little opportunity to properly train and organize the recruited men for battle. It could take a long time to collect even the most basic equipment, and it was incredibly difficult to move the armies around the country with no transport and only the most rudimentary of roads.

While still in control of his kingdom and collecting the unpopular "ship money" from his people, Charles had invested heavily in the Royal Navy. Unfortunately for Charles, in January 1642 a large number of Navy men declared themselves for Parliament. Parliament's control of the Navy would be a significant factor in their success in the subsequent civil wars, not least because it prevented Charles from blockading London to force its surrender.

The first major battle of the English Civil War was the Battle of Edgehill, fought in October 1642. Essex had hoped to force Charles into battle in Nottingham, but as Royalist forces led by Charles' nephew Prince Rupert began to move towards London, Essex was forced to attack at Edgehill in the Warwickshire Plain. The two armies were almost equally matched in number, but Royalist forces had a slightly stronger cavalry. Fighting was brutal but also confused and drawn out. Officers had neither maps nor any way of keeping time, so organizing tactics was extremely difficult and both sides were forced to improvise. Royalists and Parliamentarians suffered massive casualties; as the sun went down and the battlefield grew dark, the remaining soldiers simply stopped fighting. The armies camped side by side for the night and at daybreak the Earl of Essex returned to Warwick, chased by the King's cavalry, a technicality that gave the Royalists the right to claim the Battle of Edgehill as their victory.

Three weeks after the Battle of Edgehill, Essex and his Parliamentarian forces reached London, where he was received as a victor. But Royalist troops were only a week behind them, having taken Broughton Castle, and attempted to storm Windsor Castle on their way. Lessons had been learned after the Battle of Edgehill; Parliamentarian forces had been surprised that the King had managed to raise an army to challenge their own. Meanwhile the King had seen first-hand the horrors of war, losing loyal officers in the battle. With new perspective both sides agreed to open negotiations to avoid further bloodshed.

Sadly it wasn't long before all negotiations were taken off the table: Royalist forces attacked the town of Brentford on the north side of the River Thames and advanced on Turnham Green. The Parliamentarians saw this attack as a treacherous act but were nevertheless prepared for battle. Almost 24,000 Parliamentarian men stood with the Earl of Essex on the south side of the River Thames. By comparison Charles' army had drastically diminished in number and his men were deathly tired after their long march south.

The second battle of the English Civil War was more like a stand-off. Seeing that they were outnumbered, the Royalist army eventually retreated. Charles retired to

Oxford where he would remain for the rest of the war. At this time the House of Commons passed an Ordinance imposing a property tax on the inhabitants of London, later extending this tax to all counties under Parliamentarian control. Parliament also confiscated Royalist property all over the city of London and levied a new excise tax on its people. With all of these sources of income Parliament managed to build a huge war chest with enough wealth to fund the army and navy throughout the rest of the war. Charles, on the other hand, had to rely on donations and any money he would levy from the country around Oxford.

As the conflict moved into 1643, rather than clear-cut pitched battles with an obvious victor, the clashes between Parliament and Royalist armies grew fragmented and uncertain. In the West a Parliamentarian army was raised independent of Essex's forces. A general named Sir William Waller advanced from Winchester to Dorset and Gloucester and took Tewkesbury on the River Severn. Despite having just 1,300 men at his disposal, Waller was able to control the whole of the west of England. At the same time in Yorkshire, Parliamentarian forces were able to take Leeds but were defeated by the Royalist Earl of Newcastle who retained the North and pushed Parliament back to Hull, which refused to surrender to them.

In and around Oxford there were a number of clashes between Parliamentarian and Royalist forces. In early July, Essex raised a sizeable army and marched them from Windsor towards Oxford. The Parliamentarian army laid siege to Reading, which quickly surrendered, and advanced on Oxford's defences. While Essex's army attempted to ~~blockage~~ *blockade* Oxford, Prince Rupert returned with his Royalist forces and crossed the Thames, unnerving Londoners and mortally wounding an important Parliamentarian colonel. Essex was disturbed by his failure to defend London and offered to resign from his command, but his offer was declined.

The Royalists were gaining ground and managed to defend the north against repeated attacks. In the west too Royalists enjoyed a clear success at the battle of Stratton in north-west Cornwall, where they are thought to have been outnumbered two to one. The same infantry went on to fight a bloody battle at Lansdown, north of Bath, and just eight days later clashed with the same Parliamentarian enemy at Roundaway Down. At both battles the Royalists were victorious, but the effort had cost them dearly; they sent word to Oxford that reinforcements were needed. Prince Rupert himself answered the call and arrived in the west with fourteen regiments under his command. The strengthened Royalist army laid siege to Bristol, the second most valuable port in the country, on the 26th July and forced the governor to surrender. By the first week in August, Bristol, Gainsborough, Lincoln and Stamford had all been taken by Royalist forces. The king enjoyed a brief moment of triumph.

Charles kept the city of Oxford as his headquarters. From there he oversaw the war that was tearing his kingdom apart. Now Charles had strong pockets of support in the north and west of England and in Wales, while Parliament controlled most of the south and east of England, including London. London was then - as now - the financial capital of the whole kingdom; its allegiance to one side or the other would be critical in the final outcome of the war. If Charles wanted to win this war, his Royalist forces must capture London.

London was not completely unified in its support of the Parliamentarian cause. In August 1643 there were a number of demonstrations in London calling for peace in the kingdom. The government resorted to violence to quash these demonstrations, which were mostly led by women, and a number of people are thought to have been killed. At this point it seemed as though the Royalists might actually win the war for the king, but by autumn of 1643 the Parliamentarians decisively gained the upper hand.

On the 10th of August the King, against the advice of his nephew Prince Rupert, laid siege to the town of Bristol. The governor in charge of Bristol refused to surrender, and after a month of assaults a Parliamentarian rescue army arrived on the scene, forcing the Royalists to withdraw. Prince Rupert was determined to bar the Earl of Essex and his army's return to London and managed to get ahead of them, inserting Royalist forces between Newbury and London. If the Earl of Essex wanted to return his army to London he would have to fight his way through.

At 7am on the 20th September 1643, the Battle of Newbury began. The Parliamentarians orchestrated an offensive attack which the Royalist cavalry was, at first, able to withstand. The Battle of Newbury raged on for almost 12 hours, during which time Charles I's Secretary of State Lord Falkland was killed. Charles called a council of war and was told that the Royalist army's gunpowder reserves were almost completely drained. Seeing no alternative, Charles and his army retreated to Oxford, leaving the way open for Essex's army to return triumphantly to London.

Chapter Four

The First English Civil War:
The War Spreads

"If York be lost, I shall esteem my crown a little less…"

—King Charles I

English Parliamentarian John Pym, who would die in December of 1643, spent the autumn of 1643 - and the last few months of his life - negotiating an alliance with Scotland. English commissioners met with the Scots in Leith in August and over the course of ten days drew up a document known as the Solemn League and Covenant of 1643. This important document contained the terms of an agreement between the Scottish and English kingdoms to fight against King Charles I as one.

Under the Solemn League, citizens of the kingdoms of England, Scotland and Ireland, living under one king, swore to preserve the Church of Scotland and to reform the religion of England and Ireland. The Scottish were hoping to unite all three kingdoms with conformity to one religion; theirs. The English were hoping to gain the upper hand against the Royalists by utilizing Scotland's impressive military. Both sides got what they wanted, and on the 25 th September the final version of the Solemn

League and Covenant was officially accepted at a meeting at St Margaret's Church in Westminster.

In January 1644m\, a huge army of over 21,000 Scottish soldiers marched into England at a huge cost to Parliament. Charles was convinced the Scottish would remain faithful to their king and could not believe they had betrayed him, but this faith in the Scottish had not deterred him from forging an alliance with the Irish.

On the 15th September 1643, Charles ordered a cessation of hostilities in Ireland in the hope that he might bring any English soldiers, currently fighting the rebel Irish, back to England to join his Royalist army. In November troops began to arrive in England from Munster and Leinster and were strategically stationed to defend Chester in the west and Hopton in the south.

Through the winter of 1643-1644 a number of skirmishes took place with neither side claiming a clear upper hand in the war as a whole. The Royalists managed to take Winchester in Hampshire and Arundel in Sussex, and the Parliamentarians abandoned Reading. On the other hand the Parliamentarians took the strategic point of Newport Pagnell in Buckinghamshire and, after victory at the battle of Winceby, took Lincoln.

By the spring of 1644 the Parliamentarians had defeated the last Royalist stronghold in Lancashire and the Royalists had defeated the last Parliamentarian stronghold in Cheshire. England was divided almost equally between the two sides with no end to war in sight.

Until, that is, the Scottish army arrived. The north-east of England had been a Royalist stronghold since the beginning of the war and was held firm by the Earl of Newcastle. The Scottish army forced Newcastle to reinforce the garrison of the town before retreating through County Durham to the ancient capital of the north, York. In the meantime the Scottish army had joined up with Parliamentary forces, fresh from battle in Cheshire and Lancashire, and were preparing to attack Newcastle's stronghold in York.

Laying siege to the medieval city of York was no easy task. York was a fiercely fortified city with an inner and outer moat and a number of defensive forts. Newcastle knew that he had enough food and ammunition to last a month or more and settled in for a long stand-off. The Parliamentarian army knew that they could not blockade the entire city of York, even with the Scottish and Fairfax army surrounding it, and invited the Earl of Manchester to contribute his army to the siege.

Unable to penetrate the thick city walls with any of their weapons, the Parliamentarian forces intended to starve the city of York into submission. Confident that the King would send help soon enough, Newcastle had no intention of surrendering - but unbeknownst to Newcastle, the Parliamentarian army had been digging tunnels under the fortified city and were poised to attack. One quiet Sunday morning in June, Parliamentarian forces exploded one of York's towers and created a breach in one of its walls. Despite leading his men directly into the breach, the Parliamentarian general at the helm of the operation was unsuccessful, as Royalist garrison troops outnumbered the attackers and were able to push them back. Of the 600 Parliamentarian soldiers that attempted to storm through the breach in the city wall, it is thought that over 300 were killed.

Elsewhere the Royalists were outnumbered but not yet beaten. Prince Rupert moved through Lancashire, recruiting new soldiers to the king's cause. Once Rupert had enlisted as many men as he could, he took orders from the King to march immediately to York. So important was the fortified city that in a letter to Rupert Charles had written, "If York be lost, I shall esteem my crown a little less…"

Having received word that Prince Rupert's army was on its way, the Parliamentarian forces surrounding York marched out to Marston Moor, four miles west of York, to meet it. Prince Rupert had pre-empted this move by the Parliamentarians and took a circuitous route that involved crossing the River Ouse twice in order to surprise his enemy. On arrival in York, Prince Rupert met with Newcastle and his top generals in order to relay the orders of the King: all Royalist forces must go into battle immediately to win back York for the king. The Royalist army marched out to meet their enemy at 4 AM the next morning, the 2nd of July 1644.

Both sides fell into position, but as Prince Rupert was still waiting for more reinforcements to arrive from the south the Royalist army planned to hold their defensive positions and delay their attack until the next day. The prince was convinced that the Parliamentarian army would do the same and wait until daybreak on the 3rd to start the battle proper. However, the Scottish commander-in-chief, the Earl of Leven, was of the opinion that a summer's night was as long as a winter's day and launched an attack that very evening.

Outnumbered by as many as 7,500 men, the Royalist forces were surprised by the Parliamentarian's late attack and were unable to launch an effective defense. In just two hours the battle was over and the Parliamentarian army was victorious, something that historians have since credited to the superior tactics of General Oliver Cromwell. Prince Rupert had managed to escape the disastrous battle with his life and attempted to gather his remaining troops, but the Earl of Newcastle, unable to live with the shame of defeat, went into voluntary exile abroad.

The Parliamentarians may have won the Battle of Marston Moor but they were yet to win the war. As they made their way into Cornwall with the intention of taking the whole of the south-west from the King, Charles himself was waiting for them. The King had 16,000 men at his disposal, compared to the Earl of Essex's 10,000, and called for his surrender. The Parliamentarian general refused, but when it became clear that the Royalist army had a clear strategic upper hand 2,000 Parliamentarian soldiers escaped and the rest surrendered. The Royalist army took no prisoners and instead allowed the surrendered Parliamentarians to re-join their cause in Plymouth and Southampton. However, the beaten infantry were afforded neither food nor shelter by their Parliamentarian allies and of the 6,000 men who set off for Plymouth and Southampton only 1,000 made it alive.

By the time the two armies met again at the second Battle of Newbury on the 21ˢᵗ of October both sides were half-starved, exhausted and desperate to see this war to its end. The battle is generally described as a victory for the Parliamentarians, as the king was forced to retreat, but just a fortnight later Charles had again taken up his winter quarters in Oxford. The Royalists also managed to hold Donnington Castle, which was an important stronghold and contained cannons and much-needed provisions.

The two sides were in a stalemate, paid for in the lives of the English, Scottish, and Irish. For either army to completely crush the other, a whole new approach was needed.

Chapter Five

The First English Civil War:
A New Model Army

"I'd rather have a plain, russet-coated Captain, that knows what he fights for, and loves what he knows, than that which you call a Gentleman and is nothing else."

—Oliver Cromwell

The dawn of 1645 marked the end of an era for the Church of England. The church's key text, The Book of Common Prayer, was abolished in favor of a Presbyterian directory of worship and, in an act of Puritan revenge, the Parliamentarians sentenced Archbishop Laud to death for treason. On the Royalist side there was also disquiet as the king demoted his principal military advisors and relegated a number of his commanders.

The Parliamentarians were in control of the north-east of England and had been victorious at Marston Moor, but they had also been outwitted at the second Battle of Newbury. What's more, Charles had managed to successfully raise an army for his cause amongst the clans of the Scottish Highlands and had occupied Perth and Aberdeen in Scotland. The Parliamentarians realized that if they were going to defeat the King and make it stick they must recruit a new army and lead it with a new commander-in-chief.

Oliver Cromwell suggested that, in the interests of turning over a new leaf, all members of Parliament that held military posts should resign in one unifying self-denying gesture. All previous accusations of incompetence and corruption would thus be left in the past. After months of arguments over the particulars of this arrangement a "Self-Denying Ordinance" act was passed, and the formation of what would be known as the "New Model Army" was agreed.

In a final last-ditch attempt to bring the war to an amicable end both sides met in May 1645 to discuss a peace agreement. Parliament demanded that Charles agrees to a number of harsh terms, insisting that he acknowledge Presbyterianism as the official religion of England and that he allow Parliament to take sole responsibility for the army, navy and any further military action in Ireland. Predictably, the king rejected these demands with scorn and the war was resumed.

Cromwell's New Model Army was made up of 22,000 men in eleven cavalry regiments, twelve infantry regiments and one regiment of dragoons. This army differed from those that came before it in a number of ways. Thanks to the Self-Denying Ordinance act, pushed through Parliament by Cromwell, army leaders were banned from holding a seat in the House of Lords or the House of Commons. For the first time in England there was a clear divide between the army and the state. The New Model Army was made up of full-time professional soldiers, some recruited as veterans of the civil war and some newly-conscripted. Now managed centrally, the organization of the army was improved and the soldiers enjoyed the benefit of regular provisions. Finally, the New Model Army was location independent. Rather than being tied to a particular county or garrison, the entire army was able to fight anywhere they were needed in the two kingdoms of England and Scotland.

Cromwell was appointed Lieutenant General of the Horse in June 1645, a notable exception to the Self-Denying Ordinance he had insisted upon. Cromwell recruited only protestant soldiers and stuck by his original intention that military proficiency rather than social standing would see members of his army rising through the ranks.

The New Model Army entered the battlefield around May 1645. Charles was still determined to win the west of England for the Royalists and sent his army to lay siege to Taunton with his son Charles II, aged just 15 at the time, as Captain-General. In response Lord Fairfax, who was now General of the New Model Army, marched a huge army of 16,000 men to relieve Taunton. The siege was abandoned before this huge army even arrived and so began a series of complicated and confusing near-misses. The authorities on both sides kept changing their minds about which armies to send where, which towns to defend and which towns to attack.

On the 30th May, as Parliamentarian forces laid siege to Oxford, Prince Rupert's Royalist army stormed Leicester in the hope that it would draw Parliamentarian forces away from Oxford. The attack was particularly brutal, and although Leicester surrendered almost immediately, the city suffered a huge loss of life. The bodies of women and children were found amongst the dead.

Days after the fall of Leicester, the New Model Army gathered its troops and set out to catch the King's army off-guard at Naseby, a small village in the centre of England, close to Daventry. The Royalists entered the battle offensively, despite knowing that they were outnumbered. The New Model Army consisted of around 14,000 soldiers, while some historians believe the king had just 7,500. Charles' army was loyal but much of the cavalry were so tired of war they were almost mutinous, while Cromwell's men were fresh and inspired by religious fervour. On the other hand, Charles' army was mostly composed of long-serving veterans whereas the New Model Army was still very much new.

After around three hours of fighting the Royalists were outnumbered, outflanked and militarily outwitted. Charles and Prince Rupert left the battlefield and retired to Leicester, leaving the majority of their infantry free to surrender. Around 5,000 men were taken prisoner, a huge number considering between two and three hundred had died in battle, and Charles' remaining royal artillery was captured.

Even now the King refused to surrender and was cheered on by the success of Royalist forces in Scotland, who had managed to claim victory over an army of Covenanters at Auldern and Alford, twenty-five miles from Aberdeen. The King knew that the only sensible course of action open to him in England would be to head west and try to replace the infantrymen he lost at Naseby with new troops from Ireland and Wales. The New Model Army was hot on his heels, and by July they arrived in Dorset with the aim of defending Taunton, which was still under siege from Royalists. On the 10th July 1645, The New Model Army destroyed the remnants of a Royalist field army at Langport and Prince Rupert tried to convince the King to surrender.

Forever optimistic, the King refused and moved into the fortified castle of Ragland in south Wales, where he plotted to raise a new army from Wales and Ireland. Despite continued success in Scotland, Charles had little hope of making a recovery in England. On the 11th of September, Rupert surrendered the valuable town of Bristol; soon after, Montrose and his Royalist army in Scotland were finally defeated.

Knowing that his cause was lost, Charles insisted that his son, the future King Charles II, leave England for France to join his mother. Then, in disguise, Charles left Oxford for the final time and infiltrated the headquarters of the Scottish army in Southwell, between Nottingham and Newark. There he surrendered himself. The King was taken by the Scots to Newcastle upon Tyne where they intended to pressure him into accepting Presbyterianism as the dominant religion in England and to agree to the harsh propositions being put to him by Parliament in London. Charles refused to do either and is thought to have spent his days in Newcastle playing golf and chess.

The Scots held Charles captive, but that did not stop him from plotting his next move. Charles knew that the alliance between Parliament and the Scots was a fragile one, dependent on a number of political deals that could fall through at any time, and remained confident that he would eventually reclaim his throne. Eventually, in January 1647, the Scots handed Charles over to the Parliamentarians for a hefty fee. He was placed in captivity at Holmby House in Northamptonshire.

Chapter Six

The Second Civil War

"Blood it defileth the land, and the land cannot be cleansed of the blood that is shed therein, but by the blood of him that shed it."

—Book of Numbers, XXXV.33

The first English Civil War had reached its end. King Charles was held safely in captivity, but Parliament couldn't relax. The new rulers of England still had to complete the difficult task of demobilizing their huge armies. Cromwell's New Model Army was unwilling to disband freely. They were owed money for one thing, and had enjoyed two full years of marching around England, fighting, pillaging and living on "free quarter". Parliament gave the New Model Army two choices: either return to civilian life or serve in the ongoing conflict in Ireland. Neither option was very popular.

The unwillingness of the soldiers to return to civilian life, disagreements between Parliamentary leaders over how to handle the situation, reluctance on the part of the House of Commons to pay soldiers what they were owed, and a lack of proper compensation for widows and orphans of the war created an atmosphere of discontent and mutual distrust across England. Charles took advantage of the chilly atmosphere between Parliament and their army and, by extension, state and society, to negotiate his release. Playing for time and hoping to return to the public arena, Charles accepted some of Parliament's modified proposals. Charles agreed to surrender control of the militia for ten years and to accept Presbyterianism as the official religion of England for five, hoping something would come up to stop these promises becoming reality.

In the meantime, Charles negotiated a secret treaty with the Scots, promising to meet their religious demands. On the 27th December 1647 Charles signed an agreement known as "The Engagement" with a number of leading Covenanters. At the same time Charles was promising English Parliamentary leaders that he would tolerate religious dissenters he also promised the Scots that he would suppress these sects.

The situation between Parliament and the English military was not improving, and in October 1647 Oliver Cromwell gave a three-hour speech in the House of Commons urging the army and Parliament to make peace. It soon emerged that Charles had been negotiating with the Scots and promising reforms in exchange for their invasion of England. The English army and Parliament closed ranks and demanded that the King be placed under tighter security.

Although Republicanism was gaining strength in England at this time, many ordinary citizens in England still believed that a country must have a monarch at its head. Many others were dissatisfied with growing Puritanism in England and ill-feeling about Parliament's treatment of the English military after the war refused to abate.

Parliament's inability to restore peace and prosperity to England in the year following the end of the first English Civil War made it easier for Charles to stage an uprising. In the spring of 1648 a number of small Royalist rebellions occurred all over the country. Parliamentarian troops stationed in Wales were still unpaid and used this grievance to change sides. In April 1647 the colonel in command of Pembroke Castle declared for the King and "The Book of Common Prayer", arousing the support of most of the county. In May, Royalist rebels began to mobilize armies in Surrey and Kent but these were quickly put down by the Parliamentarian army at the Battle of Maidstone on 1st June. Essex Royalists under the command of the Earl of Norwich had recruited a large number of supporters, and the Parliamentarians found themselves engaged in a long and unexpected siege in Colchester.

Meanwhile, in the North of England, Scottish troops had begun their pro-Royalist invasion of England. The Scots, headed by the Duke of Hamilton and his army of Royalists, entered England in the west and took a route through Cumbria and Preston to reach Manchester and North Wales. At this point the Scots and Royalists in the north amounted to almost 20,000 men. Cromwell led a Parliamentarian army of around 9,000 to meet Hamilton's Royalists in Preston with the aim of cutting them off from their Scottish base. An incredibly successful strategy employed by Cromwell's superior army saw the

Royalists beaten in just four hours. Parliamentarians then occupied Preston town and chased any remaining Royalist soldiers south where, close to Warrington, they were either killed or taken prisoner. The remains of the Scottish cavalry made it as far as North Wales but finally Parliamentarian forces caught up with them; on 25th August 1647 they surrendered.

The siege of Colchester was similarly unsuccessful. Royalist forces that had escaped the Battle of Maidstone were joined by the Royalists of Essex and swelled to a force of almost 4,000 men. Caught in the town of Colchester, this Royalist Army was faced by a Parliamentarian force of over 5,000. Charging through the city gates, the Parliamentarian army lost 700 soldiers and were driven out of the town by the Royalist defense. A long and bitter siege ensued with the council of war in Colchester only agreeing to surrender on the news of Cromwell's victory in Preston.

The surrender of Colchester marked the end of the second English Civil War, but it was only the beginning of what Parliamentarians referred to as "some satisfaction of military justice". Two of the main Royalist military leaders at Colchester, Sir Charles Lucas and Sir George Lisle, were shot for their part in the second Civil War. Other executions followed. Most of the Royalists who had fought in the first Civil War had sworn not to take up arms against Parliament and hadn't, so those who had broken their word were dealt with without mercy. The Duke of Hamilton, the Earl of Halland and Lord Capel were all executed at Westminster on the 9th of March

1648. Parliamentary authorities also sentenced to death Major-General Rowland Laugharne, Colonel John Poyer and Colonel Rice Poyer, leaders of the Welsh rebels, but killed only Poyer. These executions were not the most controversial thing Parliament did following the Second Civil War, though - that notorious day was still to come.

Which ? Poyer ,

The experience of not just one civil war but two had devastated England. Many lives had been lost, families were left destitute and much of the kingdom's treasury had been spent. It is now estimated that the English Civil Wars cost proportionally more lives than the First World War. Tax levels were high, soldiers were still unpaid and took what they could from ordinary citizens, and everyone wanted to see the bloodshed come to an end. Following the failed Royalist uprisings of the second Civil War and a Scottish invasion, Charles had made himself unpopular with the English public and Parliament debated whether to return to the King to power at all. From the Isle of Wight the King continued to negotiate and intrigue with the Irish, yet even those who supported Charles tried to encourage him to retire quietly. Charles' religious stance remained unpopular in some circles, with claims that his religious policies and actions looked alarmingly like popery. The idea that Charles had provoked God's wrath and must be pay in blood for his waging of war against his own people became commonplace.

Furious that Parliament continued to barter with the disgraced King, the people's grievances turned into rebellion; the English military marched on Parliament. It seems at this time that both Fairfax and Cromwell, victorious leaders of the Parliamentarian army that won the second Civil War, were swept along with the tide. Neither were keen to see the King officially deposed, but they could not stop an army seeking justice. In a dramatic coup d'etat in December 1648 the army conducted "Pride's Purge", a radical purging of Parliament. 45 Members of Parliament were arrested, 146 were denied entry to the chamber and a further 160 voluntarily removed themselves. This left only 75 members to take part in what became the trial of Charles I.

Following Pride's Purge, a preacher is said to have quoted The Book of Numbers, XXXV.33: "Blood it defileth the land, and the land cannot be cleansed of the blood that is shed therein, but by the blood of him that shed it." On 1st January 1649, the Rump Parliament of those 75 remaining members instituted a High Court of Justice for the sole purpose of putting King Charles I on trial for treason. On the 17th January 1649, King Charles I of England, Scotland and Ireland was found guilty of treason and sentenced to death by 69 members of the court.

Three days later in front of the Banqueting House of the Palace of Whitehall, addressing a group of men gathered around the scaffolding on which he would he be executed, Charles said:

"Truly I desire their (the people's) liberty and freedom as much as anybody whomsoever; but I must tell you their liberty and freedom consists of having government those laws by which their life and their goods may be most their own. It is not by having a share in government…"

Charles I was beheaded, but the Stuart dynasty was not destroyed. Charles' eldest son, the Prince of Wales, was in exile in Holland and was now 19 years of age. On receiving news of his father's execution the young prince went to Jersey where, on 17th February 1649, he was publicly proclaimed King Charles II. Charles II immediately began to plan the reclamation of his throne, setting into motion a series of events that would bring about the Third Civil War.

Chapter Seven

The Third Civil War

"Truly England and the church of God hath had a great favour from the Lord, in this great victory given us."

—Oliver Cromwell, 1644

Following the execution of King Charles I, the remnants of the House of Commons claimed full sovereign rights in England, an arrangement they named a "Free Commonwealth". Charles II and his exiled court now had to find a way to regain the throne of the Stuarts in Whitehall.

It was unlikely foreign aid would be able to help the young king. In Holland Charles II had been a respected guest but his main ally, Prince William II, had recently died; as the United Netherlands came to be ruled by an oligarchy, he could find little help there. Charles II's mother was the aunt of King Louis XIV of France, but as France was at war with Spain it could not afford to involve itself in English matters as well. The Spanish, fearful of the English naval might, also refused to help Charles II, and so the only course of action for the King was to open negotiations with Ireland and Scotland.

Following the execution of Charles I, England was as divided as ever before, with many turning to the Royalist cause out of sympathy for the martyred king. The execution had also served to galvanize Scottish and Irish support for Charles II; the Scots were outraged that the English Parliament had taken it upon themselves to execute a Scottish monarch, and the Irish Confederates were determined to secure their independence from English Parliament. Just two weeks before Charles I was executed, a treaty had been concluded in Kilkenny between Royalists and the Irish, whereby the King had agreed to the free exercise of the Roman Catholic religion and the independence of Irish Parliament in exchange for an army of 15,000 men.

Before Charles II could make it to Ireland to pick up where his father had left off, Oliver Cromwell had arrived in Dublin as Lord-Lieutenant and Captain-General of the English army. Cromwell was hell-bent on punishing the Irish for the rebellion of 1641 and was determined to crush any Royalists still living there. On the 15th August 1649, Cromwell's army effectively slaughtered the Confederate-Royalist opposition. With confusion and disunity at the center of the Confederate-Royalist coalition, Cromwell was able to defeat the Irish in just nine months. On the 3rd of September 1649, Cromwell's forces decimated the garrison at Drogheda in Leinster and went on to capture the Irish Confederate capital Kilkenny in March 1650. At the fall of Galway in 1652, the Irish resistance was all but over; the last Confederate Catholic troops surrendered to English Commonwealth in mid-1653.

On hearing the bad news from Ireland, Charles II entered into serious negotiations with the Scottish. In

Ireland, substantial numbers of Englishmen fighting for the Royalist cause had switched sides. Irish natives who had survived the slaughter were terrified; it would be impossible to raise another army for the King in Ireland. Seeing no alternative, Charles II went to the Scottish to hear out the stringent terms for their support. After six weeks of diplomatic negotiations Charles II signed a draft agreement known as the Treaty of Breda on 1st May 1650. In the treaty he agreed to impose a Presbyterian system in England, to forbid the Roman Catholic religion across all three kingdoms and to recognize the legality of the Scottish Parliament. On the 1st January 1651, Charles II was crowned the King of Scotland at Scone, near Perth.

Charles II's arrival in Scotland did not go unnoticed. On the very day he landed the Council of State in London was debating whether or not to invade Scotland as a precautionary measure. Despite having been united as one kingdom for almost three hundred years the Scots were always regarded as enemies by the English. With Charles II on Scottish soil the Council of State saw no alternative but to launch a "preventative war" and ordered Lord Fairfax to invade Scotland at once. Fairfax refused to bring war on the Scots, citing the outstanding Solemn League and Covenant of 1643 as a reason to keep the peace. With Fairfax refusing to take up the command, Cromwell took his place; on 2nd July 1650 led an army of 22,000 men over the River Tweed. By August Cromwell's army had surrounded Edinburgh, intending to cut the city off from the rest of the country, and on the 3rd September Cromwell won a massive victory over the Scots in the

Battle of Dunbar. The English army is thought to have killed around 3,000 Scots that day and took a further 10,000 prisoner, around half of the entire Scottish army.

It was a terrible defeat for the Scottish, but in the aftermath of the tragedy Charles II was able to revive Scottish Royalism, stoking the fires of hatred between the Scottish and the English and gaining many sympathizers in northern England. Royalist organizers began secret preparations, and Lancashire Royalists were promised help from the Scottish army if they could rally the English gentry to the King's cause. English Presbyterians too began to forge alliances with the Royalists, and two Presbyterian ministers were executed on Tower Hill for allegedly being sympathetic to Charles II. Meanwhile in Scotland Charles II was accepted as commander-in-chief of the Scottish army, which was slowly regaining strength with the addition of Engagers and Highlanders Clans.

The major campaign of the Third English Civil War was launched in earnest on 17th July 1651 when a force of 1,600 Englishmen crossed the River Forth and defeated the Scottish at the Battle of Inverkeithing. Cromwell followed with his whole army and made for Perth. At this point the Scottish army had two options: try to fight the English where they stood on Scottish soil, or to march ahead to England and rally Royalist support there. Charles II pushed for the latter and the army marched across the border – reportedly covering three hundred miles in three weeks – finally reaching Worcester on the 22nd August.

Charles II had been confident that reinforcements would come to his assistance as soon as he arrived, but few

Englishmen came to his help. The Lancastrians, on whom Charles II had thought he could rely, were certainly Royalists but felt no love for the Scottish and were alienated by their presence on English soil. Attempts to recruit soldiers to the King's cause in Wales were fruitless and few from the Midlands offered their support.

When Cromwell arrived to face Charles II at Worcester, he had an epic army of around 28,000 men at his disposal. This army surrounded the city of Worcester; the king watched in dismay from the tower of the cathedral as Cromwell's forces smashed through his army's defences. The battle lasted around three hours, during which scores died. Around 4,000 Scots were taken prisoner and Cromwell claimed victory, describing it as a "crowning mercy". The very first skirmish of the first English Civil War had been fought at Worcester and so had its very last. Charles II escaped the battle and spent 45 days trying to escape England and evade capture by every soldier or citizen who might like to claim the reward. Eventually he escaped to mainland Europe, where he would spend the next nine years of his life in exile.

Conclusion

It is interesting to consider what might have happened if the first English Civil War had never come to be. If Charles I had never involved England in the Thirty Years' War, never began raising taxes without Parliament's consent, never tried to reform the church along Catholic lines, never gone to war with the Scottish Covenanters - if Charles I had agreed to all of the restriction and demands of Parliament - could civil war have been avoided? It is impossible to know, but it is certain that England and Great Britain as a whole would be a very different place today.

The English Civil Wars made a number of irreversible changes to life in England. Firstly, the crown lost its feudal rights and authority over the courts. Secondly, the crown lost its right to levy taxes without Parliament's consent or to arrest Members of Parliament without cause. Thirdly, Parliament became a permanent part of the British institution and lastly, the Church of England ceased to be the sole religious institution.

There are no verified figures for how many lives were lost during the English Civil Wars, but as in most wars of the period more lives were lost to disease than in actual warfare. Historical records count over 84,000 people killed in conflict with over 100,000 more killed by disease in England alone. No records were kept of Scottish soldiers killed in the wars, but estimates suggest another 60,000 people may have died in Scotland and in Ireland. Where plague, Irish civil war and famine added to the death toll from the English Civil War, it is estimated over 600,000 people died - 40% of the pre-war population.

These wars were the last civil wars to be fought on English soil, but sadly not the last to tear Ireland and Scotland apart. The three kingdoms that fought in the English Civil Wars were forever changed by the struggle, learning lessons about power, religion and freedom that still resonate today.

Made in the USA
Middletown, DE
01 February 2023

23565061R00029